Mike Peyton

Quality Time?

fernhurst
BOOKS

First Published 2005 by
Fernhurst Books,
Duke's Path, High Street, Arundel,
West Sussex, BN18 9AJ, UK

British Library Cataloguing in Publication Data.
A catalogue record for this book is available from the British Library.

ISBN 1 904475 20 5

Printed in China through World Print.
Artwork and cover design by Veronica Gates.
Edited by Simon Davison

For a free, full-colour brochure write, phone, fax or email us:
Fernhurst Books, Duke's Path,
High Street, Arundel, West Sussex,
BN18 9AJ, Great Britain.

Phone: 01903 882277
Fax: 01903 882715
Email: sales@fernhurstbooks.co.uk
Website: www.fernhurstbooks.co.uk

By the same author:

'An Average War'

'An Average War' tells of Mike Peyton's experiences in a Recce battalion with the Eighth Army in North Africa. It tells of his capture and then his escape from a German PoW camp, and of his reaching and fighting with the Red Army on its advance to Berlin.

£10 including p+p from: Mike Peyton, Rookery Cottage, North Fambridge, Essex. CM3 6LP

Acknowledgements

These cartoons were first published in
Practical Boat Owner and *Yachting Monthly* magazines

Dedication

TO:

- [ ] Skip, to show there are no hard feelings
- [ ] The Crew, to show there are no hard feelings
- [ ] My husband; remember me?
- [ ] The mate; remembered for extreme tolerance
- [ ] The winner of the ....
- [ ] The Chairman of the Handicap Committee
- [ ] The Chairman of the Protest Committee
- [ ] The navigator, who finally got us to ....

  ....

- [ ] The foredeck, who learned to love

  anchoring/spinnakers/picking up buoys/ ....

  ....

  ....

(tick where appropriate)

Contents

1. Fifty Years of Sailing 5
2. Deep Water 38
3. Land in Sight 49
4. All Ashore 62
5. Jumbles 77
6. Below Decks 83
7. Stopped for the Moment 86

'Tea up skip.'

1

Fifty years of Sailing

When you work as a freelance and your publisher says write a few words on how you became a yachting cartoonist, you write. So here we go.

I drew my first cartoon, and others, for a wall newspaper in a German prison camp. I went over the wire shortly afterwards and had no time to continue this line of work when I joined up with the Russian army, but that cartoon was a

Probably the first cartoon I drew

portent for the future. With the war won, a grateful government was giving grants for further education if you were able to prove interrupted training owing to the past hostilities. As all Adolf Hitler has interrupted in my case was two evening classes on drawing a week, I applied for a grant with little hope of success. But fate, or I think it was, was on my side. During the war I had served in the Western Desert in what the press of the day called the Desert Rats, but which we knew as the 'effing Mickey Mouse Club'. My particular unit was the recce battalion of the 50th Northumbrian Division where I entered the battalion's efforts on the situation map, us in red and them in black.

As I also carried the map, where the C.O. went I went too, like Mary's little lamb. As he was very enthusiastic I sometimes thought he pushed our luck a bit too far. However, I survived but he didn't. Sometimes in those distant days we went to what were called 'conferences' where a few officers met in the vastness of the desert and conferred, and one of these officers, with a photographic memory I assume, was on the board of examiners who saw me to decide if I might be a suitable candidate for Manchester Art School. Whether his recognising me swung the day I have no idea, however we did exchange a few words about these momentous times during a coffee break, so I doubt if it did me any harm. And so I became an Art Student and was taught how to draw.

The yachting bit took a bit longer.

After a year at Manchester I transferred to a London Art School - which was fine except that my grant was based on my living at home. If as an art student I did not actually starve in a garret, I was often pretty hungry on the third floor up. I scrubbed out pubs etc. to earn the wherewithal to live and pay for my digs and I often hitched home were the food was free. It was these trips home and the conversations with lorry drivers that gave me the ideas for cartoons for magazines such as *Commercial Motor.* And it was also at this stage I drifted imperceptibly into sailing.

England was on its uppers in those post-war days and many people were selling up and leaving the country. I met a man in a pub in Richmond who was emigrating and I bought a canvas canoe off him. It was about twelve foot long, with a twelve-foot mast and leeboards. The upper reaches of the Thames soon palled and gradually I worked my way downstream. At night I generally slept on moored lighters and I remember once frying breakfast on the primus, overlooked by Big Ben. Eventually I arrived in salt water and learned to reef and found out about tides the hard way.

Then there is a big gap in this learning curve, as I got married to Kath my long-suffering wife. Many years later I was sailing down the Thames on a Thames barge and I pointed out to the skipper the saltings opposite the Chapman light and I told him I had spent the first night of my honeymoon there. His reply was, "You must be effing joking!" Obviously he was very unimaginative and couldn't visualise the full moon and huge fire of driftwood in the shelter of the seawall. However, that was the last trip we had in the canoe as we were on our way to walk in the Alps, and we followed the usual procedure of handing it over to someone to look after and use until we returned. In this case to the Tonbridge Sea Scouts. We never returned to Tonbridge so, who knows, it may still be there?

After a few yeas of work, and travelling in Europe when we had the money, we thought that before we settled down we would have one last fling and decided on a trip working our way across Canada and back across the States. One of the best interludes on this journey was a canoe expedition into the bush in Northern Ontario. Planning for this I visualised all the tins of food we would need and, even worse, all the dollars we would need to buy them and thought there must be a better way. Then came the thought, what did the old time trappers do? They had no supermarkets and Toronto library had the answer. The old trappers lived off what they termed the three "B's": bacon, beans and bannock (a primitive bread made of flour and water). The only decision to be made was the size of the side of bacon and the size of the sacks of flour and beans. I mention all this because years later when I was running a charter boat I tried to get my charterers to accept the balanced nutritious diet bit but they demurred. With hindsight I realised the only way one could work up an appetite for this basic food was to spend a full day paddling a canoe with the odd break of a couple of miles portage of a seventy pound craft.

Back in England we drew a circle around London, where I knew my work would be. The circle had a fifty mile radius and we went house hunting wherever the line crossed a river. Subconsciously something was working. With impeccable timing Kath was left £800 and with that behind us we found and bought a derelict cottage. It had no floors or unbroken windows, but for £750 what could one expect? But we ignored the drawbacks: it was only a few minutes walk from a tidal creek in the upper reaches of the River Crouch. Though I did not realise it at the time, we had arrived.

It was the creek and its boats in their mud berths and their owners that immediately attracted me. The boats, like their owners, were a motley collection: an old smack whose buyer recouped the price he had paid for her in the eels he found in the mud inside her bilges; a barge yacht whose owner told the tale of racing a mattress down the river to Burnham but was beaten because the mattress got a better slant in Cliff Reach; a lifeboat conversion bought for a song because its owner hadn't come back from the war. There was even a live-aboard on an old bridging pontoon. They were as a whole a subspecies of the yachting world emerging from primeval mud. They bought their yachting gear from the outlets with the self-explanatory name of Army Surplus Stores. When I bought my first boat and with the previous owner sailed it back to the creek, I fitted in like an oar in a rowlock. I would come over the sea wall in the winter and look to see which boat had a smoking chimney - for they had solid fuel stoves - and that's where I would go for the first cup of tea of the day.

Obviously the only thing that stopped this crew having proper yachts was a shortage of money. But they were all getting around that in their own way for they all had a boat of some description. The lifeboat conversion was a case in point. Britain then had a huge Merchant Navy and all their ships carried lifeboats which, in accordance with Board of Trade regulation, had to be renewed after a certain period of time – so the end result was obvious. There were about three standard sizes of them and they had a ready market. In fact there was a popular book of the time titled *Lifeboat into Yacht* and you would often see the end results of people who had read this book out sailing, and realise how the various owners had interpreted it.

There was one specialist lifeboat on which I had a worrying trip across the Thames Estuary. It had been designed by Uffa Fox to be carried under an aircraft and dropped to aircrew who had come down in the sea, sitting in their little rubber liferaft hundreds of miles from land. Because of the constrictions in design, such as being carried under an aircraft, it had very little freeboard. This had been improved by fitting it with an inflatable tube all around the gunwales. The trip I had in one was worrying because the owner had got rid of this inflatable tube and the freeboard was measured in inches. I thought at the time that the only thing this was good for was rinsing the teapot.

My first boat had been what was known as a penny sick, a 24 foot open gaff-rigged centreboarder with eighteen inches draught. In its working life it had taken holiday-makers to the end of Southend pier and back. When I bought it someone had built up the topsides and decked it over, covering the deck with lino. It cost me £200 and left us with £3 in the bank. Kath told me later that because of this impulse buy she didn't speak to me for a week, but what annoyed her was that I was so excited by buying the boat that I never noticed. However she got over this and later spoke, proudly I like to think, of having the only gaff-rigged kitchen in Essex.

But my biggest disappointment at this time was that I couldn't sell any yachting cartoons, though I could easily get half a dozen ideas, often based on doom and disaster, just getting out of the creek. What I didn't realise then was that yachting in those days, as written about in the yachting magazines, was a serious business. Yachtsmen wore peaked caps and put white covers on them, navy fashion, on the day that was ordained as the start of summer. Ensigns came down on the dot at sunset. Paid hands were only just disappearing. I went on boats where the only access to the forepeak was through the forehatch where the paid hand had lived with the paint and sails.

I can date the first sail I had in *Vagrant* (I called her that because she had no visible means of support) by the other world shattering events that were happening at the same time. One of them was the Hungarian revolution. It was because of this I also got my first crew - many people had to leave Hungary in a hurry and people were asked to take them in and we got Gabor, a student. So on our maiden voyage there was Gabor who was keen but couldn't speak English and hadn't even seen the sea (he'd flown in at night) and Tommy, an unflappable ex-army friend of our desert days whom I discovered by chance was a near neighbour.

So we three tyros set off on our maiden voyage, the plan being to sail to the mouth of the Crouch and back. We had on board a copy of one of the finest books in the body of English literature – *Sailing* by Peter Heaton. If Heaton had one fault it was to advise his readers to eschew the engine until they could handle a boat under sail. I'm very good at eschewing and as the engine wasn't working it was only too simple. Peter Heaton had pride of place on the engine case where Tommy and I had frequent recourse to the information he had to offer, and Gabor had his new English Hungarian dictionary to flip through and a roving commission with the boathook.

We ran down the Crouch with the prevailing south westerly behind us and the ebb tide under us in a state of bliss, and it was only when we got to Shore Ends that we found we hadn't quite the experience to sail back against the wind and tide. Later we found that a previous owner had removed the bowsprit and this had completely unbalanced her. We didn't know enough to anchor and wait for the flood, so kept on doing what we had been doing since we set off, running before the wind. Our shoal draught kept us afloat as we ran up the coast over the sands. The weather worsened as we sailed north and at one time I had a cutting from the local paper – and of which I was inordinately proud – which said racing had been cancelled on the River Blackwater because of the weather conditions. We had a panic when Gabor, who most of the time had been clutching his lilo and being sick, flipped through his dictionary and pointed below saying, "Puddle, puddle!" Looking below we saw the floorboards were awash and every time *Vagrant* pounded, the centreboard case grew two watery ears where the centre bolt was. We learnt a lot on that trip from *Vagrant* and Peter Heaton but the first thing we did when we got into West Mersea was to sort out the engine.

Vagrant continued to teach me a lot as is the way with your first boat and Peter Heaton, who had ended up as pulp in the bilges, was replaced and now shared the bookshelf with Maurice Griffiths and later Eric Hiscock. These two authors influenced a generation of yachtsmen: it was either Essex creeks or distant horizons. Personally I am pleased I plumped for the former.

Later I realised that on our maiden voyage we had sailed through a bombing range, because most of the area between the rivers Crouch and Blackwater at that time were so designated. It was marked by four DZ (dropping zone) buoys. Later I, and other East Coasters, had many a heated argument with the American crews of the motor boats in which they rode shotgun over the areas. They were heated because they tried to prevent us, often engineless gaffers, from going through the Rays'n Channel into the Crouch. The alternative they had in mind was through the Wallet Spitway, then further east than its present position. It was about seven miles with a fair tide through the Ray'n, as against fifteen miles with at least half this distance stemming a tide through the Spitway.

'It's civilisation alright Bob. I can read the signs: Supermarket, Petrol, Restaurant, Topless......'

The East Coast was now our oyster and *Vagrant*, generally with its distinguishing flag hoist of drying nappies (we now had two daughters, Hilary and Veronica), made the most of it. Both Kath and I have a joint memory of sharing the Pyfleet with seven working motormen. Motormen were barges who had struck their topmasts and shipped their bowsprits which distinguished them from the few real sailormen left. I only saw two sailormen working under sail, *Cambria* and *Anglia*, which was actually taking a tow down to the Swin from a motorman. Perhaps this was symbolic.

Even more symbolic was the last time I saw Bob Roberts, the skipper of the *Cambria*. He was in the Plough and Sail in Paglesham keeping the customers, both locals and visiting yachtmen, happy with his squeeze-box as he must have done often in the past in waterside pubs of the East Coast. He was belting out "A is for the Anchor", "Stormy Old Weather" and all the old traditional East Coast songs. He had stopped for a drink when a pretty young girl came up to him and asked for a request. It was a request for a song and it was a song from another world, one that had been made popular at the time by Nancy Sinatra. The title was "These Boots are Made For Walking". Bob finished his beer, closed up his squeeze-box and left.

Then came the day when, looking at *Vagrant* from the shore as oft times in the past and thinking that I must be one of the luckiest men in the world to own such a fine vessel, I found faults. I had outgrown her. I sold her to a banana importer from Birmingham. Part of the deal was that I delivered her to the London end of the Grand Union Canal. Because of this I am occasionally reminded of her when locking into St Katharine's Dock. On this delivery trip I planned to lower the mast at St Katharine's but this was my first trip up the Thames and I found that although St Katharine's was marked on the map, it had not operated for years. Only the help of a river police boat and a friendly tug boat skipper saw *Vagrant* in her new cruising grounds.

There were times when the denizens of the creek, of whom I was now a paid-up member, would go down to the Ferry Boat Inn at Fambridge for a drink where we would rub shoulders with proper yachtsmen who paid to keep their boats on swinging moorings and sailed to foreign parts. It was here in the bar I had got to know pretty well that I overheard a conversation that had lasting implications for me. The speaker had just come back from Holland where, because of the polderisation, he told of rows of sailing fishing boats going for a song in the fishing harbours around what was then known as the Zuideer Zee.

I hadn't many pounds at the time but what I had were then rated as hard currency. A few weeks later I owned an ex-Dutch fishing boat, E B 49, a 40 foot Botter with a 13 H.P. Kromhout diesel. It had a fish well and all its gear and I paid its wooden-clogged owner £400 for it. The botters all looked alike to me, but this one was varnished and all the others were tarred, so that was how I chose it out of many. I worked on the assumption that if he was keen enough to varnish his boat this would be reflected in the rest of his boat, and so it seemed. He even gave me the recipe for his varnish.

There were three of us who went to Elburg to collect it: Gordon, who had most experience as the nominal skipper, John, who had lots of sea time but which was discounted as it had been on an aircraft carrier, and myself to sign the cheque. We sailed on November 5th. I did consider calling her Guy Fawkes but the sail Number 49 led to forty niner and his daughter Clementine and so I called her *Clementine* and forgot the "Sank beneath the foaming brine" bit.

We were bound for Amsterdam and due to some oversight – probably excitement – we hadn't provisioned the boat. We arrived in Amsterdam absolutely famished and by sheer luck found a taxi in the dock area. It is difficult to believe now, but then not all Dutch taxi drivers spoke English. We reverted to sign language by rubbing our stomachs - whether we rubbed too low down or he jumped to conclusions, whatever it was we were delivered to a brothel. However the Madam took the loss of business quite well and sorted it all out including arranging for the driver to deliver us to a restaurant and, even more important, ensuring he would pick us up after the meal, as only he knew where the boat was.

Most people have a memory of some exceptional meal and on this trip I had mine. It started by my being as sick as I have ever been in my life. There wasn't a retch left in me as Gordon and John nobly stood my watches. Then came the time I realised I was over it and staggered weakly outside to take the tiller. Before Gordon went to his bunk he asked if I wanted anything, to which I replied "Food." "Dry bread?" was his query. "No, food!" was my reply. He later returned with a frying pan full of what is covered by the phrase Full English. There were sausages, bacon, eggs, beans, tomatoes, fried bread and a large spoon. Steering by leaning on the tiller I started shovelling it down. As I was doing this he returned with a mug of tea which he placed on the large gimballed antique compass (it was at least eighteen inches across) which was in a box at my feet, then he left me to it. Only a yachtsman can appreciate what such a meal meant. It was then I also realised how lucky I was. There was I, master before God of this fine vessel with a fair fresh wind on the quarter and brown sails straining above as we rolled homeward bound across the grey North Sea. Below was sleeping a trusty crew with whom you could sail the seven seas. I can assure you, at that moment I would not have called the king my uncle.

Back in England *Clementine* proved her worth as she was ideal for the East Coast with her shoal draught and the ability to take the ground. All her gear was simple and basic and pretty near unbreakable, though heavy. You pumped her out, if that is the correct term, with a shovel. This shovel had high sides and fitted almost exactly in a channel in the bilges by the fish well and if you worked quickly enough – in fact you had to – you could scoop up a shovel full of water and get rid of it into the fish well. She is the only boat I have sailed in where I came under unfriendly fire. It was a dark night and I was chugging up the Crouch on the tide when two friends of mine appeared rowing out of the darkness in a large dinghy. "Just the man we want," they said as they climbed aboard and made the dinghy fast. I could tell immediately by the alteration in the engine note that they had been – and now I was – towing a drudge for oysters. No wonder they had been happy to see me, but nothing was said. What could I say? They were friends. Then shortly afterwards out of the darkness we heard shouting and cursing from the sea wall and a shotgun was fired in our direction. However, luck was on our side and we got back to the creek unscathed. Peter, one of the pair who lived just over the sea wall, provided us with an early breakfast. The meal which came up was angels on horseback. I did not know then but I do now that these are oysters wrapped in a slice of bacon and I have to admit they were very good.

Mediaeval as she was in most respects, *Clementine's* leeboards had an aerofoil section, and she also had rod rigging. In fact the only rigging she had was an iron bar for the forestay. But on the whole she was labour intensive. In fact the regular crews, nearly all ex-servicemen, had a saying that three trips on *Clementine* entitles one to a Botter Campaign Medal. Nevertheless a lot of people had a lot of pleasure on board her, although the communal bunk – it was 12 foot wide – was never popular. I cannot recollect the details of her sale but I received an offer and I decided to go for something smaller which I could handle alone with Kath and the two children.

The day before the new owner was due to come and take *Clementine* away I went down to the creek and on going aboard found her leaking. There were two clearly defined jets of water coming in on the port side opposite the mast.

When the tide had left her I shovelled the water out and, putting on my gumboots, waded through the mud and hammered some caulking back in. The following day we were having coffee with the new owner prior to the handover and as a point of interest he told us the previous evening he had been at a party in South Kensington where he had been talking to someone who was considered to be able to see into the future. In the conversation with him he mentioned he was buying a boat and received the amazing reply, "I can see it now. Looking at it from the front it is very big and brown," – a perfect description of a varnished botter – "and on the right side of it opposite the mast there are two jets of water coming in." I choked on my coffee.

By now a keen yachtsman (my wife said besotted) and influenced no doubt by reading every book on sailing or cruising the local libraries had to offer, I spent the money I got for *Clementine* and bought a 30 foot Colin Archer, a double-ended gaff cutter with the odd name of *Sugar Creek*. She had a tiny cockpit, barely a footwell, and I had to put another bottom in it as otherwise the cockpit was so deep you went in it up to your armpits. There was a 7 H.P. Sleipner petrol paraffin

'I generally give them an hour to get comfortable before I wake them and tell them they can't lie there.'

engine which you primed on petrol and then switched over to paraffin. Her solid construction had many advantages and one, in those pre-marina days, was that she could be left in any harbour to rough it out with the fishing boats. Harbours were then considered places of refuge which gave one a different attitude to them and they were generally free. As we had no car to anchor us, we left her where we fancied. We always had a train timetable on board and as trains were punctual and frequent we travelled down to the boat and returned home by train. I remember getting her as far west as Brixham using this method. In those times the yacht club secretary often rowed out to welcome you – those were the days!

I bought *Sugar Creek* from a Mormon who explained that her odd name was the site of a Mormon skirmish. She was always referred to as *Sugar* by us. In her I was able to move to a swinging mooring at Fambridge as the idiosyncratic character, Old Mick – Meiklejohn was his proper name – who ran the moorings there wouldn't take any boat, or owner for that matter, that didn't meet his critical approval. He liked *Sugar* – "Not one of them bladdery things." He slipped up once with his judgement of character but won out in

'Admitted, there's a few bills outstanding, but it was when he said he didn't trust me that I decided to leave.'

the end. A customer ran up a large yard bill and decided to leave during the small hours on a favourable tide but Old Mick had finally read him right. As he pushed himself out of his mud berth he was brought up all standing by the length of chain shackled around his propshaft and then to a pile of the mud berth walkway.

At this time Kath my wife was earning money writing children's books and I was also earning by doing commercial art on a freelance basis. But, more to the point, about this time I sold my first yachting cartoon. One weekend I sailed to Calais with the editor who bought it. He had been involved in the Dunkirk debacle and as we sailed into Calais he pointed to the lighthouse and told me, "The last time I was here I was on the top of that with a Bren gun."

Moving to a mooring at Fambridge was a big step up in my sailing life for in its way, because of Old Mick's partialities, it was more exclusive that the Royal Yacht Squadron. I could now consider myself a yachtsman. Apparently Old Mick who had retired from a life at sea as an engineer in the Merchant Navy had been sailing around the East Coast looking for a suitable business to retire to and, according to his wife, when he sailed into the Fambridge moorings he looked around and said to Mrs Mick, "This will do." He was no fool and chose well. It must have seemed idyllic, just twenty or thirty moorings with the low slopes of the Crouch valley beyond the roofs of the village (the pub being the closest) and what was always referred to as The Shed on the sea wall. This had been a prefabricated hospital building in the Crimean War but now it was The Shed, built out on piles over the river overlooking the moorings. Here was the hub of the moorings and at the end of a weekend a large pot-bellied stove would be keeping the kettle boiling and if you had been accepted into the inner circle, a long process I assure you, you would partake of tea as the doings of the weekend were discussed. This gathering in The Shed was also an important feature of the Fambridge moorings as it was always expected that one would pick up one's moorings under sail and obviously the earlier arrivals would watch you do it. You were judged by your peers. It certainly concentrated the mind on the wind and tide as you approached your buoy and you would know by which boats were on their moorings who the audience was. However, it evened itself out over the year and it was very satisfying to know when you had done it well that you had an appreciative audience, not that any mention would be made of a superb bit of boat handling. Though on the other hand even a slight misjudgement might be obliquely referred to.

The shed would empty gradually on Sunday evenings with reference to train times and your walking speed, as the station was a mile and a half away. Few owners drove.

This process was reversed on Friday evenings when the train from London came in and weekend supplies, which had been ordered by postcard, would be collected from a small wooden general store situated just on the limits of high water. The store would often be closed but there would always be a row of cardboard boxes marked with the boat names: *Charm, Reedbird, Radiance, Merlin, Salad Days* etc., waiting to be collected. Later in fact when I read her obituary in the local paper, I found out that the wife of *Salad Days* had been the WAAF driver for Bomber Harris during the war.

In the winter the boats were moved into mud berths and it was there that they became the meeting place for the hard core who came down during winter weekends. Like the boats in Clement's Green Creek, they all had coal stoves on board and over the weekends these stoves never went out. As in Clement's Green Creek, if a chimney was smoking you would be welcomed on board – though the boat that got the most visitors because of her size and comfort of its cabin was a forty-foot Bawley named *Gladys,* which had been one of the boats that had picked troops off the beach at Dunkirk.

Obviously some work was done on board over the weekends but, whatever

'Pity about the weather skip, when we're all psyched up for a weekend's work.'

job was in hand, it stopped in the evening when we congregated in the Ferry Boat Inn and set the lamps a-swinging. There were always a few locals in the pub but one that was invariably in his regular corner was Reg Watson the ferryman. He had done time in the Navy but in the 1914-18 War he had skippered a Thames sailing barge running coke from Beckton Gas Works to Calais. He told me once how over forty barges had left Calais on the tide for Beckton, and the obvious race had ensued. His barge, the *Westmorland*, was one of the smallest but was the second barge home.

During the '39 War he had been coxs'n on an Air Sea Rescue launch operating on the Thames. His relief coxs'n was now the landlord of the pub at Heybridge Basin and their job had been to pick up pilots who bailed out. He told me that during the blitz on London if there had been a rough night in the East End, where Reg came from, they never saw any German pilots at all: they simply left them to drown. When Reg died, the ferry died with him.

One of the pleasures or perks of Fambridge came about after Old Mick considered you competent enough to deliver boats that were moving onto or off the Fambridge moorings and whose owners, unbelievably to the eyes of half a dozen of us, did not want to deliver them themselves. They were generally weekend jobs, though we did sail a King's Amethyst back from Gdansk in Poland. We were lucky in this case as though it was a brand new boat its keel fell off a couple of days after we got back when it was on its moorings. We would have missed that if it had happened in the middle of the North Sea. Another delivery trip was of a steel Dutchman with eighteen inches draught. I remember it because we set a course from the North Foreland to the Crouch, a distance of about 23 miles as the crow flies., and went over every Sand between: the Margate, the Tongue, South and West Shingles, the Barrow and the Maplins, all possible because of the shoal draught. Normally when sticking to the channels and swatchways it would be almost double that distance. For an East Coast yachtsman it was pretty unique.

On one delivery three of us had anchored off Dungeness to wait for a tide and the anchor chain jumped out of the fairlead and because of the prevailing conditions it was busily sawing off the bows before it was sorted out. I never had to look far for cartoon material. More often though the boats we moved were elderly wooden boats. Two of three of us would clamber on board on a Friday night curious to see what we had got, and as we swept a torch around the boat probably the only shiny thing we would see on board was the pump handle.

Only occasionally did we get to deliver boats with hemp halyards, which were then considered to be the height of luxury. No money changed hands for these trips, not even expenses; we just did it for the pure pleasure of sailing another boat.

It was at Fambridge that I also joined a club. A few of the younger boat owners had started sailing in company. It was noticeable that most of the boats of the members of the yacht club were home-built of marine ply by their owners. An Evenide, a Lightcrest and two Buccaneers come to mind and they were generally engine-less. The club was a very nebulous arrangement and in the main consisted of being flexible, in fact that became its name: The Flexible Yacht Club. If on the previous weekend a few members had agreed to visit the Medway, and on the following weekend the wind was from the south west, it would be pointless turning up looking for members of the F.Y.C in the Medway as it was assumed you would be flexible enough to turn up somewhere in the Harwich area where the fair south-westerlies had blown you. A fair wind was the operative phase. We even had a burgee: it was for Heineken Beer, an advertising handout that could be obtained for the asking at most garages in Ostend.

The trip across the North Sea to acquire this burgee was also considered necessary to be a fully paid-up member so we flew it with pride. Though there was a day when the club secretary of Torbay Yacht Club rowed out to greet us on a windless day, and just as he asked me what club I was a member of and looked up at the burgee a whisper of a breeze came up and all was revealed. The letters F.Y.C. on the transom of most of the boats I draw in my cartoons had their origins, as did many of those early cartoons, in the Flexible Yacht Club. It also had a flagship because the owner of the King's Amethyst we had delivered was not all that keen on sailing and left it to one of the delivery crew to maintain and use as he pleased. The skipper, a generous character called Jimmy Green, was ex-navy and after emigrating to New Zealand after the war had returned to the U.K. because he said all they talked about was sheep and rugby. Now he had free rein on this 33 footer and as both he and the two regular crew liked a drink it probably did more duty free runs than most boats in the moorings. They often took their wives with them, probably for their duty free allowance, and their system was to give their wives a sleeping tablet each for the trip across.

Nineteen sixty was a year seared on the memory of my sailing days as this was the year I almost lost *Sugar* and my family. We were beating down the Barrow against a fresh south westerly bound for Whitstable, where we were going to stay with friends of our student days, when suddenly all the rigging went slack. Later we assumed the mast had not been right down in its mast step and as this was the first sail of the season the movement had shaken it home. I dropped the sails and went to start the engine until things were sorted out. But the engine wouldn't start, due to the magneto, the curse of marine engines of the time. A winter laid up in the airing cupboard was the norm for magnetos but this time it hadn't done the trick. By now the Barrow Light Vessel had sent up a flare to warn us we were in danger of being carried onto the sands so I pulled up the staysail and retraced my course, running with the wind. After tightening up the rigging I considered the wind was now strong enough to warrant a reef and while doing this the sail split. Harwich now became our destination, about thirty miles away. With hindsight I should have attempted to go through the Wallet Spitway but then hindsight is like that, and I kept going to the end of the Gunfleet Sands. By then I was too far east with the ebb under me to slant Harwich. I found out later that other boats were in trouble that night as the Southsea-Harwich Race was on and *Yachting World* had a report saying because of the weather conditions sea sickness was rife amongst the crew, four boats were pulled in by the lifeboats and one yacht was reported as making morse with difficulty. This was crewed by four offices of the Royal Corp of Signals. However, this did not solve our problems and though not life-threatening at that time, off the Cutler Kath put her Girl Guide training into use and flashed up S.O.S. at a passing ship. I had told her that if we kept on going as were we would end up in Norway and quite understandably she said no, not with the two children on board.

The ship was a train ferry and although it gave us the lee the swell was such that as its substantial rubbing strake dropped it first took off our spreader and then it opened up the deck. One of the crew took his life in his hands and, held only by his belt by two of his mates, leant down and took first Hilary and then Veronica off from me where I was standing on the doghouse. Aged four and three, they both took it quite well, telling the crew they had been shipwrecked just like Rupert Bear. The water was over the bunks by the time I got off and *Sugar* was abandoned. I will always remember that not one person told me how stupid I was for going to sea with such a crew. However, *Sugar* was a wooden boat and she still floated, though now she was considered as a hazard to shipping and as such she was towed to Harwich by a Trinity vessel, and later taken to Walton where she was repaired to be sailed again.

It was in the refitting that I decided to have a pulpit. It was considered a bit sissy by many to do so but with time we were learning sense. We already had pig-netting round the aft end of the boat to keep the children from falling off. (Chandlers had not cornered the market in yachting gear in those days and farmers' suppliers were often very useful.) The day I fitted the pulpit was one I always remember as I had collected the pulpit from the galvanisers, rowed it out to the boat and offered it up. I was below in the forespeak fitting it when one of the regular crew rowed out and, assuming the pulpit was fitted, decided to use it to pull himself on board. Instead of arriving on board he ended in the water and the pulpit at the bottom of the river. However, both problems were catered for by the gear of the times. He sorted himself out by getting on board by the bobstay and the bow sprit whiskers and the pulpit we fished up with the dinghy anchor. In those pre-marina days of swinging moorings and anchoring off, a dinghy and its small anchor were essential equipment. So the day was saved and the two of us fitted the pulpit together.

Many of my winter evenings at this time were spent with other sailing friends attending navigation classes, not as common then as now. We could easily go to three in a week, driving a fair distance to do so, and as this was long before the breathalyser came into use we generally had very jolly evenings. It was to put the information we had absorbed into practice that a long trip was planned by four

'Better take your Quells, dear, school's out.'

of us the following summer. The destination chosen was San Sebastian in Spain and the reasoning was simple. If you turn left at Ushant and steer approximately south-east you will ultimately see land. If the land lies north and south you go south; if it lies east and west you go east and whichever one you chose you will arrive at San Sebastian. As we did. We did have some outside help as regards our navigation that wouldn't happen nowadays. Two fishing boats made a detour out of curiosity to speak to us and when they left we took a bearing on their course. As they were registered BB we transferred the bearing from Bilbao onto the chart working on the theory of Riq, who was a Catholic, that they would be going home to celebrate the Feast of Assumption. And so it proved.

On the outward trip we had six days out of sight of land which was the most any of us had ever done. We also had the saying 'When the sea hog jumps stand to your pumps' proved to us. There was an evening when the dolphins started leaping high out of the water and as darkness fell the weather worsened as their actions foretold. But one thing *Sugar* could do was heave to – in fact, jokingly, we considered it her best point of sailing. We put a light in the rigging and as we had plenty of sea room did hourly watches while the others turned in.

On the homeward trip we called in a few harbours, one being La Rochelle. It is brought to mind when I watch the reruns of the film *Das Boot,* as the massive concrete submarine pens were still as the RAF bombers had left them, piled higgledy piggledy like childrens' building blocks. Guilvinec was another harbour we called in where the French fishermen could not do enough for us. In fact their kindness had a negative side as they moved our boat so quietly that we awoke to an empty harbour and found we had missed our tide.

We returned back up the Channel in three tacks and here we experienced something that showed the passing of an era. At that time flag etiquette was an accepted part of sailing with ensigns being struck to the minute by sticklers for protocol, and dipping your ensign to a man-of-war was obviously the done thing. Coming back up the Channel we were overtaken by three French corvettes foaming past in line astern. It was raining, I was alone at the helm and it was no trouble for me to reach behind me and take the ensign staff out of its socket and dip it. On cue a door in the bridge of the leading corvette opened and a matelot emerged pulling on his oilskin before scampering astern to dip the Tricolor. The whole procedure was repeated with the second corvette. But not the third. I dipped my ensign and waited for a reaction but no one emerged from the bridge. Then a window was slid open at the side of the bridge, an arm emerged and I was given a stiff two fingered salute. The old days were going fast. We got back to Fambridge after 26 marvellous days out.

It was in *Sugar* that we entered the first East Coast Old Gaffers Race. The race from Osea Island to Harwich was bedevilled by the weather conditions. There was no wind at the start on the ebb tide and an easterly wind on the flood, so it was a drift on the fair tide then a beat against a foul tide and most of the thirty-odd competitors called it a day and retired. However we plugged on and finished fifth at 01.30 hours, one of the seven finishers.

It was also in *Sugar* that we were involved in a tragic disaster. John, who had crewed back with me in the botter and also to San Sebastian, bought a boat himself. She was an eighteen foot double-ended gaffer called *Snipe*, well known on the East coast because it had often been written about by its previous owner, the author Francis B Cooke. In fact he started one of his books by writing, 'Snipe was launched on the day of Queen Victoria's jubilee.' She was lying at Ramsgate and John and a mutual friend Jack were fitting her out there. Came the weekend when they planned to sail her to Fambridge where they intended to keep her, I sailed across the estuary to accompany them home. My crew for the trip were Kath, my wife, Tom Bolton a friend and two brothers, Dave and John Young. We arrived in Ramsgate as they were stepping the mast, a hop pole they had bought. Now with hindsight I think that was the cause of the tragedy. It was common enough in those days to use lashings instead of bottle-screws and this was the case here. The tide served about midnight and I towed them out of the harbour with Tom sailing on *Snipe*. Always keen to sail on another boat Tom, Dave and John had cut cards for the privilege and Tom had won. We crossed tacks somewhere off the North Foreland with a rendezvous previously planned off Whitstable, this being the recognised method of crossing the estuary for engineless boats, in on the flood by the Kentish shore and out on the ebb by the Essex shore. We waited in vain for them off Whitstable but we never saw them alive again.

It was assumed they had gone aground on the Margate Sands but *Snipe* was later found in two pieces, which makes me think that as the lashings for the mast got wet and shrank so the mast was forced down strongly enough to split *Snipe* in half. It seemed ironic that the three of them had survived the war, John on an aircraft carrier, Tom with the Royal Engineers and Jack as an infantry sergeant in Burma, to die in home waters. A sad sidelight on the tragedy was that Tom's dog started howling at about two o'clock in the morning which we assumed was about the time the accident happened. It was inconsolable and affected so much that a week later it had to be put down.

All three of them were members of the Old Gaffers' Association, John and Jack having crewed on *Sugar Creek* on the first race in which Tom had entered his own boat, the smack *Maria*, C.K.21. He had bought *Maria* for a pound and this was the one that had had enough eels in its bilges for Tom to make a profit on the deal. (Essex creeks in those days invariably had some old smack rotting away in them. These wrecks were a bone of contention between their owners, generally old fishing families, and yachtsmen who owned wooden boats and who considered rightly that the decaying smacks were a breeding ground for the dreaded gribble worm.) Because of the OGA connection, a few of us had a whip round and bought a cup which has been raced for every year since in the annual Old Gaffer Race, the Tom Bolton Cup. It is awarded to the first ex-working boat home. It may give you some idea of Tom's attitude to sailing to say that, after we had towed *Maria* from Tollesbury Creek off the River Blackwater (where he found her) to the Crouch, he came to the conclusion that the main beam which was in poor condition would not take the strain of the mast, a telegraph pole he had acquired, so the mast was moved forward to the next beam. Then the length of the boom was considered to be excessive. Tom's answer to this was to acquire another telegraph pole and set this up as another mast and rig her as a schooner. Probably the first and only smack to be so rigged.

How I came to sell *Sugar Creek* I can no longer remember exactly but I think I was approached and I was ready for a change. At that time a Colin Archer was considered the classic cruising boat par excellence and the buyer, one Chris Doyle, had his eyes on distant horizons. I had often brought *Sugar* back to Clements Green Creek to work on her as it was only walking distance over the fields and saltings from our cottage. By now the creek dwellers had acquired a dry dock converted from *Lillian*, a swim headed Thames lighter. As I was still a paid-up member it was in this dry dock that Chris and two friends started fitting her out for blue water. Copper sheathing was considered essential for tropical waters in those days and they beavered away happily until Chris acquired a girlfriend. Human relationships then came into play and when he sailed away she was his sole crew.

I am pretty certain they got to the Virgin Islands, as years later I saw advertisements in the yachting magazines for a pilot book of the Virgin Islands whose author was Chris Doyle. On a more depressing note a friend who had also sailed in the Virgins told me she had seen *Sugar Creek* pulled out on a beach somewhere and she was so dried out by the sun that she was past redemption.

I have owned three classic boats in my time: the Colin Archer, a Folkboat and a Vertue called *Concerto*. Regretfully I only had one sail in the latter. During my time at Fambridge I had a friend known as Scotch Bob who had an odd way of life. He had lost both his parents and kept his boat at Fambridge only because his sister had married a local man. He himself spent the winter months of the year at sea as he had his mate's ticket and then in the summer months sailing on the East Coast. He was away at sea one winter and there was a fire at the boatyard and his boat *Concerto*, the Vertue, was damaged. But even worse than that his sister had died. She had kept up his correspondence for years and the reminder for his insurance was found on her desk unopened. *Concerto* was uninsured.

Before he went back to sea I arranged to buy *Concerto* off him at his valuation and have it repaired, and then sell it, keeping the cost of the repairs and what I had paid to him out of the selling price. The stern and the cockpit had been burnt out. The insurance company then was the East Coast Mutual which was run by yachtsmen who invited those they considered good risks to become members. They turned up trumps. Hearing the sad chain of events, they paid up the full value of *Concerto*. Bob wrote saying "One good turn deserves another" and gave me the now repaired *Concerto*. I sold her to an enthusiast almost immediately and the only sail I had on her was the delivery trip down the Solent, during which I realised why Vertues have the reputation they have. It was winter and it snowed a lot of the time and my only firm memory of the trip is anchoring in the Downs in company with half a dozen coasters waiting for the weather to moderate.

As for me I bought another classic, a Folkboat. If my memory serves there were three Folkboats in the five entrants in the first single-handed Atlantic race in 1960, so what better recommendation? The one I bought, *Froyna*, was a standard Folkboat with crouching headroom and to our eyes over-powered with a 10 hp Sabb. However we soon got used to that. The evening three of us went to collect it from Walton on the Naze it was snowing, but we were so taken up with her handy performance that when we were in Harwich we spent a lot of the time taking it in turns to pick up a mooring buoy then throwing the buoy over-board and doing it again. However, much as we decried *Sugar's* unhandy ways we missed her coal stove as we shivered that night in our sleeping bags. For one hooked on winter sailing that was *Froyna's* Achilles' heel. Nevertheless, we had some fabulous sails in *Froyna*. One memorable one was when the three of us sailed her from the Crouch to Cherbourg on a Bank Holiday weekend. The wind was easterly, just on the wrong side of being comfortable and we teetered for hours on the verge of being pooped. We arrived soaked, exhausted and famished in Cherbourg just as all the restaurants were closing. However, the last one we tried took us in and we ate a magnificent meal in the solitary splendour of an empty restaurant, a meal which we at least thought we had well and truly earned.

Another sail we had was when five of us, the family and a friend, went off to the Channel Islands for the summer holidays. I remember it now because of the trip back. Somewhere north of Alderney the engine gave up the ghost. It wasn't worth even taking the engine cover off as we could hear a broken cog rattling around the gearbox. It was a windless day and the tide was sluicing us down to the Casquets. We had tied every available rope to the kedge, including the headsail sheets and the mainsheet, and still could not get to the bottom. We could think of little more to do when a light easterly wind came up and we hauled up all our warps, re-rove them and crept across the Channel, getting into Weymouth forty-two hours out from Alderney. It was the remark of the engineer who repaired the engine that I always remember. He was a member of the lifeboat crew and perhaps they had a different attitude to their job in those days but his remark, "Small diesels and big filters have knocked the bottom out of the Lifeboat business" was one I took to heart. I have had big filters ever since.

I have always had an interest in the old traditional fishing craft of the East Coast and in the Fenn Creek I saw an old Gravesend Bawley, the *Amy*, rotting away. She was said to be one of the smallest ones built at 28 feet and I thought I could salvage her. I bought her for a tenner with an old outboard thrown in, and moved her round to Clements Green Creek using a Trespassers Will Be Prosecuted notice board for a rudder. The idea was that I would take an old plank out and put a new plank back. However it was not to be. There just wasn't enough time to work on her. It seems criminal now when one sees how old boats are rebuilt to such high standards these days but then old wrecks like *Amy* were two a penny and, bearing in mind the dreaded gribble worm, we put a match to her. Something I have always regretted.

About this time one of the buzzwords of the day was the coming of the age of leisure and I decided to do something about it and cater for the leisure market and run a charter yacht. This idea had come about almost imperceptibly because as I had sailed down the Crouch on a Friday evening I had often been greeted by the owner of a boat, a large slabsided gaffer anchored off Wallasea, called *Dorothea*. He always seemed to be rowing people on board and his greeting was always the same, "Where are you bound?" I felt I should have been answering the Indies or Trincomalee or some such exotic destination, instead of Pin Mill or the Medway, but that is how I got to meet my mentor. He used his boat to take out members of the Civil Service Sailing Association and I ended up taking his overflow. My instructions were basic: I had to teach his clients how to tie a bowline, put a reef in, swing a lead and how to light a primus, which was the normal cooking stove of the time.

As the type of freelance commercial artwork I was then doing had no regular hours I reckoned I would be able to juggle both jobs, commercial art and chartering. It seemed ideal. I would be getting paid for what most people, me included, considered pleasure. It also fitted in with what a lecturer at Art School often stressed and which I had come to realise was very true, that "Design doesn't end on the drawing board" – i.e. design one's life. All I needed towards this end was a bigger boat.

I had no trouble getting rid of *Froyna* and then came the enjoyable task of finding another boat. I had done this a few times for both my own ends and with friends when they were prospective buyers and we considered it pure pleasure – looking for the boat that had that indefinable character that would lift your heart. It was invariably a winter occupation and normally there would be four of us in somebody's company car and we would set off on a Friday night with a list of boatyards to find with boats to look at and then a Bed and Breakfast in some pub on the Saturday night to round off the day as we discussed our findings.

In this way we found *Dowsabel,* a 33 foot six-berth yawl with a 18hp Sabb diesel, with a lovely sheer and a canoe stern, lying in a canal off the Humber. The present owner said the owner he had bought her from told him he had designed her himself as an amateur, but I also found that Francis B. Jones had been his neighbour, so I ignored that. I still remember the ex-owner shouting out the pilotage in the darkness as we cleared the lock at Immingham. It was the pilotage necessary to get us down into the Wash and was as basic as one could get:"Hug the mud!" And so I went into business.

My first charter party was two married couples from Northampton and by a quirk of fate I am still in contact with the couple who are still alive. Brian, now retired, lives in France but most years he and Doreen return to England and visit a mutual friend and we meet. It is forty-odd years ago since I first trained the binoculars on the four strangers in pristine yachting gear standing by the side of The Shed, wondering what was in store for them.

Dowsabel was a victim of her own success and from the outlay of the only three ads I have put out she was seldom on her moorings. So I came to think: if I can take out four people each trip why not six, or eight? The effort would make little difference and the profit double. All I needed was a bigger boat. A forty-footer?

Almost on cue, this was the time that ferro cement was the flavour of the month, with the potential for a biggish, seaworthy boat with minimum maintenance at a reasonable cost. Ferro was the obvious answer, for the hull of a ferro boat could be built much more cheaply than that of a wooden boat. GRP was under way but had not yet got the complete dominance of the market as now. Many big boats at this time were being built of ferro because it was cheap, but of course the cost of everything else, mast, sails, engine, etc. was as normal. I think one of the reasons why ferro boats got such a bad name was that many of their builders did not do any costings and, generally, because the weight of ferro construction did not lend itself to small boats. Everyone built big boats that were parish-rigged. Forty foot was about the minimum when ferro and wood were approximately the same weight, with ferro getting progressively lighter as the size increased. For me one of the greatest attractions of ferro, besides the minimum maintenance, was that you could have a one-off design that you thought would make a good boat.

We started building at the back of the house and almost immediately I was initiated into the fellowship of other builders of ferro boats. It was almost a type of Mafia with a marvellous atmosphere, with help, ideas, friendship there for the asking. The king pin in our area was a keen sailor called Aussie Edge who fortuitously worked for Blue Circle Cement and through whom we could contact their research department. At weekends we had so many visitors Kath said at times she thought she was running a coffee shop (twenty four in one weekend) and of course on plastering days, where you saw the boat take shape before your very eyes, everything ended with a party. The plastering had to be done in one hit and the more hands the better, so on plastering days every ferro boat builder within miles turned up with a conscripted girlfriend.

I had a stroke of luck when the hull was nearing completion, when I got the idea of going to visit a ship breaking yard. It sounds industrial but it was simply a few wooden minesweepers hauled out on the saltings which the sole owner and worker were breaking up. The man was filthy but he had a clean pink copy of

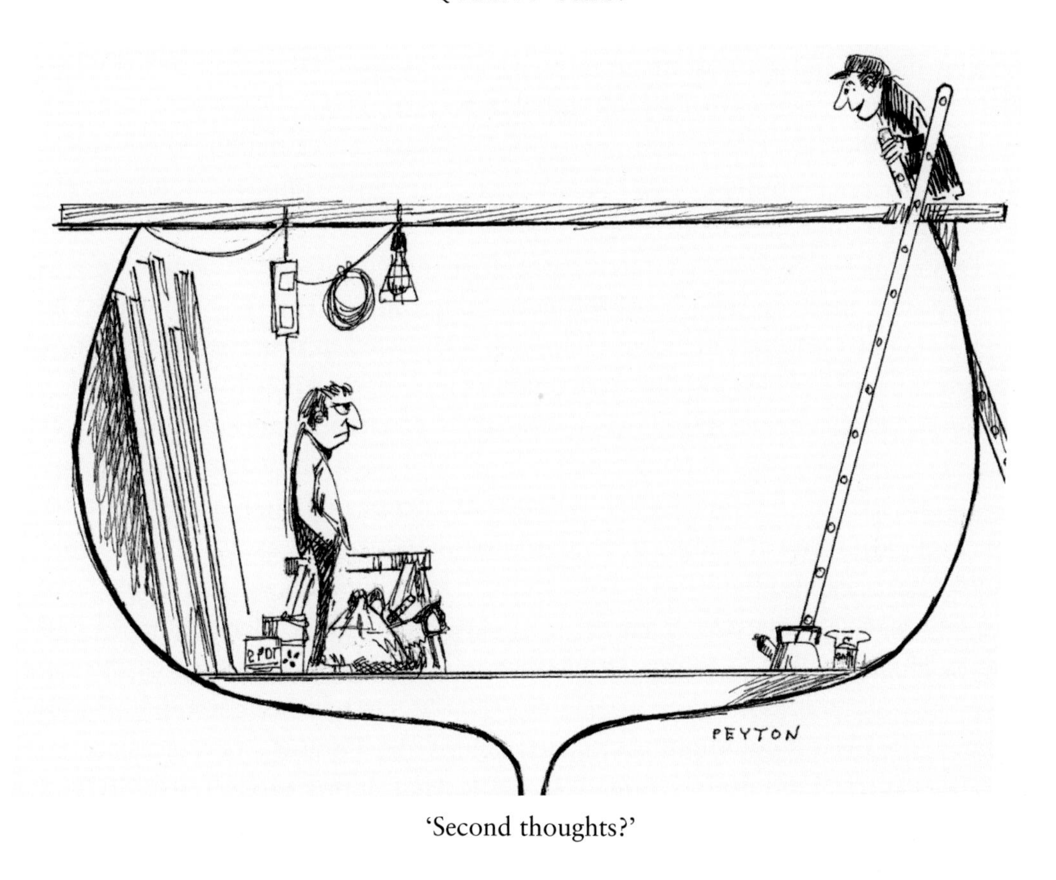

'Second thoughts?'

the current Financial Times sticking out of his back overall pocket to let him know the commodity value of the brass and copper he was salvaging. He had no interest in wood and I arrived at a critical moment as he had just set light to a huge bonfire. I bought it off him for a fiver and he kindly helped me put the fire out. This bonfire kept me in hardwood for many a long time. On my present boat I still have a mirror which he allowed me to unscrew from the wardroom bulkhead of one of the other wrecks.

When built *Lodestone* was the sum total of all the desirable qualities of the boats I had owned. Forty foot I knew I could handle and shoal draught was desirable so she had a centreboard giving her four foot draught. A small cockpit like *Sugar* – in bad weather it cannot be small enough, in good weather who cares? – it also allows for a large cabin. Large cabins generally are where the best parties are. She was a cutter-rigged yawl to keep the crew occupied, with a flush deck, a split rig, and an air-cooled hand-start Lister diesel. Paddy proof, as a charterer who was in the construction business described it. I wanted huge cockpit drains and a transom stern, as I had been pooped in both my double-enders *Sugar* and *Dowsabel*. I took my ideas to Alan Hill, a local yacht designer, and he did the clever stuff and made a marvellous job of making them work. Built like a brick shithouse, as the saying is, she was without a doubt a very successful go-anywhere boat.

Two ideas which I incorporated more than earned their keep later. One was to have steps made in the side of the stern-hung rudder. This was influenced by my hearing of a crewless boat found drifting in the Med. It was assumed the crew had gone overboard for a swim and couldn't climb back. Later I was involved in a search off the Bench Head where the man who had gone overboard was actually alongside, but his crew could not get him back on board. The steps on my rudder earned their keep when we were at anchor one night and a charterer fell overboard when attending to a call of nature. Because of these steps he could and did get back and I only found out about it when blowing my top about some clot who had left wet towels on the chart table. The other idea was one I had seen in Holland where a triangular chainplate raised the pickup point of the cap shrouds to be in line with the mast bolt in the tabernacle. It meant that as you lowered the mast it could not take charge and move about.

The first trip I did in *Lodestone* was to the Med. I have often wondered how I managed to do this trip without getting divorced. However, I did (it was a close call). Kath and the children sailed over to Calais with me where we dropped the mast and then we went through the canals to Paris where they left me, Kath insisting that the children did not miss any school. From Paris a friend named Vic Temple crewed down to Lyon and we finished off the interior of the cabins as we went along.

Vic, who had met his German wife when in the Army of Occupation in Germany, was of the Hiscock inclination rather than Griffiths and later built a Wharran cat and sailed away to distant horizons. He had enough forethought to keep up his National Insurance payments so that in later years, when he was in Maine and needing hospital treatment, it was there.

When I arrived in the Med I was alone and faced with the job of getting the 44 foot mast up. To do this I looked for a climbable tree and rammed the bows of *Lodestone* into the bank opposite it and made a line from the bow fast to the tree. I then rowed both anchors out on the quarters to hold her in position. Then the mast had to be manhandled until I could get the foot into the tabernacle and its holding bolt in place. With backstay and cap shrouds on I climbed the tree and made a block fast up high and rove the main halyard through it. I assure you all this took longer to do than write. Then came the critical point. All this time I had been watched by a number of curious silent French fishermen. I looked at them and they looked at me and I held up the end of the halyard. To a man they put down their rods and within minutes with them hauling on the line the mast was up and I was making fast the forestay.

During this trip down through the canals and the Rhone I came to realise that the French were even more enthusiastic about ferro than the British. I would hear tapping on the hull and when I stuck my head up I was invariably taken away to look at ferro boats in various stages of construction. But one visit was exceptional. I was actually in the Med at the time when I got this invitation on the ferro grapevine. Because *Lodestone* was a handsome and efficient-looking boat I was literally the guest of honour when I visited Les Frères de la Mer, the Brothers of the Sea. I sailed along the coast and anchored off and was welcomed with open arms. The atmosphere, friendliness and enthusiasm was just as with the British ferro builders only more so, for instead of individual boats there were twelve of them all being built together. Twelve hulls all waiting to go in the water. The Brothers of the Sea had formed a commune to build them. The hulls were dotted about in a clump of palm trees with the tents and shelters of their builders and families alongside. All seemed to be wearing the minimum of clothing and all were burnt almost black by the sun. There were plenty of children playing about and no shortage of dogs and cats in the camp, with the smoke from the campfires, on which they cooked, drifting up into the palms. It was a cross between a boatyard, a gipsy encampment and a scrapyard and one could almost feel the holiday atmosphere because today was the day the first boat was going to be launched. The upshot of it was it was launched and it went down by the head in no mean manner. It was a serious design fault and everyone knew there were the other eleven identical boats still ashore. I could have wept and I have no doubt some did.

I had about eight pleasant months wandering around the Med. By now I was selling cartoons regularly, sending them back to England. I had started selling articles to the yachting magazines and so I convinced myself I was actually working. Kath and the children joined me in the school holidays. The Med had fewer marinas than it now has, and invariably in the harbours I went into, even Cannes, there was a cheap end and always a bar that catered for financially handicapped yachtsmen whose boats were in these admittedly tatty areas.

In these bars I often picked up crew for the longish trips. As an example, I was approached by a young Canadian who said he had heard I was looking for a crew to Corsica. He himself was heading for Japan but by his book Corsica was on the direct route. He came on board and I found he had been a law student who had been involved in a traffic accident just after graduating. Deciding to conduct his own case he had been successful and wrote a book 'How to Conduct Your Own Traffic Case'. It had hit the jackpot and with the profits he took off for Japan. I will always be grateful to him because of something he did. I got up and as I came through the hatch he pointed to the north where there was a line of irregular shapes glistening in the darkness. When I got the glasses on them I realised I was seeing sunlight shining on the snowfields of the Alps at least two hundred miles away. I was seeing daytime from nightime. I thought at the time, "Those who go down to the sea in ships see the wonders of the Lord".

The live-aboards I met cruising around the Med were a mixed and friendly crowd but living in much smaller boats than is now the norm – a family of five in a Folkboat, two New Zealand couples in a 24-footer. But on the whole a much smaller group then, and as people left for other harbours and other boats arrived news was passed around and you gossiped and compared notes and you soon felt you knew everyone in the Med. The upshot was that when you went into another harbour or anchorage you recognised the boats and knew of the owners before you actually met, as they did of you. It was these live-aboards that introduced me to Chateau Plastic. It was wine bought from the Farmers' Cooperatives in large plastic containers at a ridiculous price and to which you added water and sugar to taste.

In Calvi I found out what had happened after the disastrous launching I had witnessed by the Brothers of the Sea. I was sitting in the cockpit when a girl sculled out to me in a minute dinghy and wearing a bikini to match. She climbed on board and introduced herself in fluent English, or American, as she had worked in an American army camp. As one who had been there on that day of ill fortunes, she told me that most of the twelve boats had ended up as houseboats, but those that had been rigged for sailing had had to be ballasted down so much that their decks were pretty near constantly awash. She and her partner were now in a small ply boat.

It was also in Calvi, where there was a large French Foreign Legionnaires' barracks, that I was approached surreptitiously in a bar by some Legionnaires to take them off the island and drop them on the Italian coast. A fair bit of money was promised but I declined as I though they might not be satisfied with an Italian beach and it might be me that would be dropped off, and not necessarily on the coast at that.

A fashion at the time was for some of the bimbos of the day to go topless. Obviously I had noticed this, particularly in Saint Tropez where it was almost de rigeur. It was also considered the done thing to wear an Iron Cross on a chain around the neck as a fashion statement. Almost anything else would have laid to such moorings in comfort but not an Iron Cross, so one's eyes were constantly riveted to its erratic movements. But perhaps that was the intention.

Obviously in eight months quite a few things happened but one incident is often brought to mind for me today when sailing on the East Coast. I had sailed into Mortella Bay in Sardinia and anchored, the only boat there and, reading the Pilot as I sat in the cockpit, I found out that the ruined tower overlooking the anchorage was the original Martello Tower. The Pilot which had been written by an ex-naval officer often added interesting snippets of British naval history and so I learned that this tower and the few men in it had held up the fleet of Admiral Hood. I rowed ashore and forced my way through the dense maquis to the ruin. With its massive construction and small entrance well above ground level the tower had held out long enough to impress the British to such an extent that when it had been taken plans were drawn of its construction for future use. The end result you know, and have probably seen, as there are plenty still standing now – on the East Coast particularly. But when I see one now I am back, however fleeting, forty-odd years and standing in those ruins under a hot Mediterranean sun, the aromatic scent of the maquis and my boat at anchor below, which I suppose is what cruising is all about.

Of the many beautiful anchorages I went into in the Med the one in the Levezzi Islands was, to my eyes at least, exceptional. The deserted islands, as they were then, sprawl between Corsica and Sardinia and could be – and have been – a death trap in bad weather. But in good conditions they are magical. As I found my way through the rocks into the anchorage I could see a mast sticking up over the farther rocks and as I let my anchor go I was pleasantly surprised to recognise both the boat and the skipper. I had laid alongside them in Lymington. That evening as we were sitting in his cockpit over our chateau plastics I was invited to dinner. My host provided that evening meal by putting on a pair of goggles and flippers, taking his spear gun and flopping over the side. He climbed back on board in a remarkably short time with two large colourful fish. I must admit I was very impressed.

Pleasant as this life was, I soon realised that sunshine doesn't guarantee good sailing or more pleasure, and the live-aboards were no more content than any other group of people. And the sailing was generally worse. The phrase 'Mediterranean rig' meant mainsail and motor and the mainsail was generally to keep some shade on the deck. I went barefooted and lived in a pair of shorts for months. I watched my anchor drop down through crystal clear water and dig into golden sands, the wine was cheap and I had some marvellous times but I realised this wasn't the life for me. I missed my family, hankered for the tides and sandbanks of the East Coast, old friends, familiar rivers and pubs I knew. Years later my eldest daughter who was working aboard boats in the Caribbean told me they had a phrase out there: "Another bloody day in Paradise". I knew that feeling then, if not the phrase, and headed for home.

Back on the East Coast *Lodestone* took to the job she was designed for like a duck to water. Winter and summer she sailed around the East Coast or shuttled across the North Sea. Calais was considered a weekend trip. I took the phrase that men and ships rot in harbour to heart. If charterers rang up mid-week, as they did, and told me they had to pull in to a layby to get some sleep before they could drive on home, I knew they would be back. Some of them still come – members from Sparkhill S.C. from the Midlands and Frampton S.C. from Gloucester were some of my first punters and are still coming. As they were dinghy club members that had, and have, a practical attraction: they have their own oilskins and know which way to push the tiller. It was the best way I knew of earning a living I could think of and the cherry on the top was the cartoon ideas I got and which I was now selling regularly. Going to work for me was rowing out to *Lodestone*.

For over thirty years I did this in three ferro boats: *Lodestone, Brimstone* and *Touchstone*, which I owned one after the other. All without accident, which is what charterers require. During this period of owning ferro boats our way of life was changed for us. The cottage we happily lived in was compulsorily purchased to make way for a new town and we had to move – happily, as it proved eventually, for the better. At the time it was traumatising. Shortly afterwards I was approached to join a consortium to buy a share in a boatyard that was up for sale in Maldon. Initially there were twelve of us, all yachtsmen, and we all moved our boats there. Four of them were built of ferro – Stonehenge was often mentioned – and as the berths all dried out we had to work our tides. But soon

I got used to that and had no regrets.

It was from Maldon that I ran the charter work for about twenty years and made many good friends in the process. One particular one was Danny Bray who normally sailed on the Humber and came to try a charter weekend in different waters. He had been in the same Division as myself during the war and became the regular mate. He had been fortunate enough to survive the entire war in the Royal Engineers, then ironically was blown up lifting mines in Germany after the war was over, which left him with a stiff leg. For a few years we had a Christmas tradition of sailing up to Wintringham Haven on the Humber where he lived, generally starting on Boxing Day, and while the boat stayed there for a while he did jobs on board. He put a bigger engine in once while I, who had got hooked on skiing, went off to stay with some Swiss charterers with whom I had come to a reciprocal arrangement. They provided the skiing in the winter and I provided the sailing in the summer. Danny and I had some very good trips together: Brest 82, Amsterdam 91, and we sailed around Britain, often with charterers joining us en route.

During this period, perhaps with delusions of grandeur and of running a vast fleet, I built another ferro boat called *Brimstone*, a 35 foot yawl. With the two boats together we sailed mob handed, 13 or 14 instead of 7 or 8. However, vast profits did not accrue, only bigger parties and bigger worries as I started developing a split personality when I stuck my head out of the hatch and could not see the other boat. Sometimes, depending on the experience of the charterers, *Brimstone* needed a skipper and the best of these was Doug Sanders, a man who during the war had skippered a naval school boat in the Thames Estuary where potential naval officers learnt their navigation. He had been one of the old hands in Fambridge moorings who had put a white cover to his cap when the Navy considered summer officially started. He still did this and his standards were high.

Good luck, as I had found out during the war, is something that never comes amiss and about this time I had some. Kath had been down to Burnham-on-Crouch where she had met John Puxley, the son of the man I had bought *Vagrant* from long ago. He was crewing on a boat in the Fastnet and they were one short. "Did I want a berth?" Though I had done a fair bit of crewing on the offshore East Anglian races I had never done a Fastnet so the temptation was great. Normally I wasn't one to let things interfere with my sailing but for some reason, probably what seemed an important deadline at the time, I declined. Was it luck? Fate? Whatever it was, the Fastnet was the notorious one in 1979. The boat

Trophy was lost and John was drowned.

My third ferro boat was *Touchstone* and Kath, who might have been getting fed up with ferro boats being built in the back garden, threatened that if I built another it would be called *Tombstone.* As I was now in my sixties there may have been some truth in this. However, fifteen years later I am still sailing in *Touchstone* which is a very versatile boat. Again Alan Hill did the clever stuff. The bottom of the hull, the cabin sole and the ballast are incorporated in four inches of reinforced concrete. With only a metre draught on 11 metres overall she can take the ground in comfort and two drop boards keep her from sagging off as they give her two metres draught when either one is down. Like the botter's lee-boards they have an aerofoil section and they are also toed-in seven degrees to help her to weather. Years ago I read that the old fishing boats struck their topmasts in winter which gave me the idea of her having two rigs. She is Bermudian rigged in winter and gaff rigged in summer, which almost doubles the mainsail area. A slide running in the mast groove takes the place of the gaff jaws and the topsail never comes off, so you never lose the leading edge. Reefing is tied in as normal on the mainsail and only one halyard is needed. With a vang from the end of the gaff to the top of the mizzen mast, which stops the gaff itself from sagging off, she has been a very successful rig though, like most of my boats, labour intensive to keep the charterers happy.

Over the years most of my charterers were from dinghy clubs but I did have other parties that were a little out of the norm. One was a photographer and three models. The idea was that I dropped them on a beach in France with nothing but the mini bikinis they were wearing, no passports, no money, nothing. Obviously the French customs officials would arrive, perhaps with luck an international incident would ensue, and the photos would sell world-wide. Sea sickness put a stopper on that idea.

A couple for a week of their honeymoon was definitely a one-off as there were only the three of us on board. A party of women from a sailing club who threatened to lash me to the mast, but unfortunately didn't, was an annual booking for a year or two. A debt collector – of all people, who refused to pay because it had been an almost windless weekend – paid up when a policeman I had on board suggested I got the firm that employed him to take on the job of collecting the money. Gary, who had first sailed with me as one of a group of ex-scouts, had ended up as a lecturer in a German university. Six of his wealthier students – they had been there and done that – told him they were bored and didn't know what to do for a holiday. Gary with his mordant sense of humour passed them on to me. They had a week which, weather wise, was one of the foulest the East Coast could offer and they had a fantastic time, or so they said. The feedback from Gary was they never stopped talking about it.

One of my last charter weekends on *Lodestone* started with a very pleasant surprise as the charter party was the four New Zealanders whom I had met in the Med. They had come over to Europe to have a year wandering around before they settled down, what would now be called a gap year. This weekend was to be their last fling before they returned home and I remember being slightly apprehensive as both girls were now pregnant, one quite heavily. I was apprehensive enough to look up the correct procedure which was all down in the Reeds Nautical Almanac. One party, all ex R.A.F. men, talked a lot of the time in service jargon: Uniform Whiskey Foxtrot Bravo Tango Sierra translated as 'unidentified wog fishing boat to starboard'. A professional after dinner speaker was another charterer I had. He knew so many jokes that he had us in stitches when he first came on board but by the end of the weekend I was seriously considering throwing him over the side if he told another one. A woman who was looking for a partner and realising she had half a dozen potential mates to consider over a weekend would have taken out a season ticket if I had let her.

A journalist got the idea that as the Royal Yacht left the Thames with Princess Margaret and Armstrong Jones aboard on the first night of their honeymoon, he would send out loyal greetings by morse on the Aldis lamp. As the Royal Yacht was delayed we drank a bit in the meantime, the message we composed and suggested he send – "This night England expects that every man will do his duty" – was only vetoed at the very last moment.

Over the years, and I did it for years, the charterers I had were a mixed bag. But on the whole a crew from a dinghy club for a week on the normal milk run, Calais then up to Ostend and back, were the best. They were out to enjoy a sailing holiday and all I had to do was point them in the right direction and hang on to their oilskins. If I had not had pound notes to prove it I would not have known it was work.

There was a period during these years when the Beatles' songs were all the go and in the discos of Ostend, where we generally ended up on these weekly trips, we must have heard them all scores of times. But one title, sung by Mary Hopkin, seems to sum it all up. It was "Those Were the Days My Friend".

And so they were, my friend, so they were.

2

Deep Water

'It's your wife. She wants to know if you're enjoying your silver wedding anniversary.'

'Decided what courtesy flag you want skip?'

'Who the hell do you think I am, Ellen MacArthur?'

'At least it shows interfacing the autopilot with a waypoint works.'

'It's only a shower, not worth coming down for.'

'Did you read that article in P.B.O. on sail trim?'

'Yes, that's it. Fully comprehensive cover...... credit card number 68059....'

'My wife thinks I'm a fussy eater too.'

'I got the idea from Baywatch.'

'Perhaps a red sky does delight a shepherd but I assure you this doesn't delight me.'

'I suppose it's some consolation that there are others as stupid as us...'

3

Land in Sight

'What d'ya mean you've changed your mind? Why?'

'I appreciate you not wanting to trouble me so early but as I'm here it's fifteen quid.'

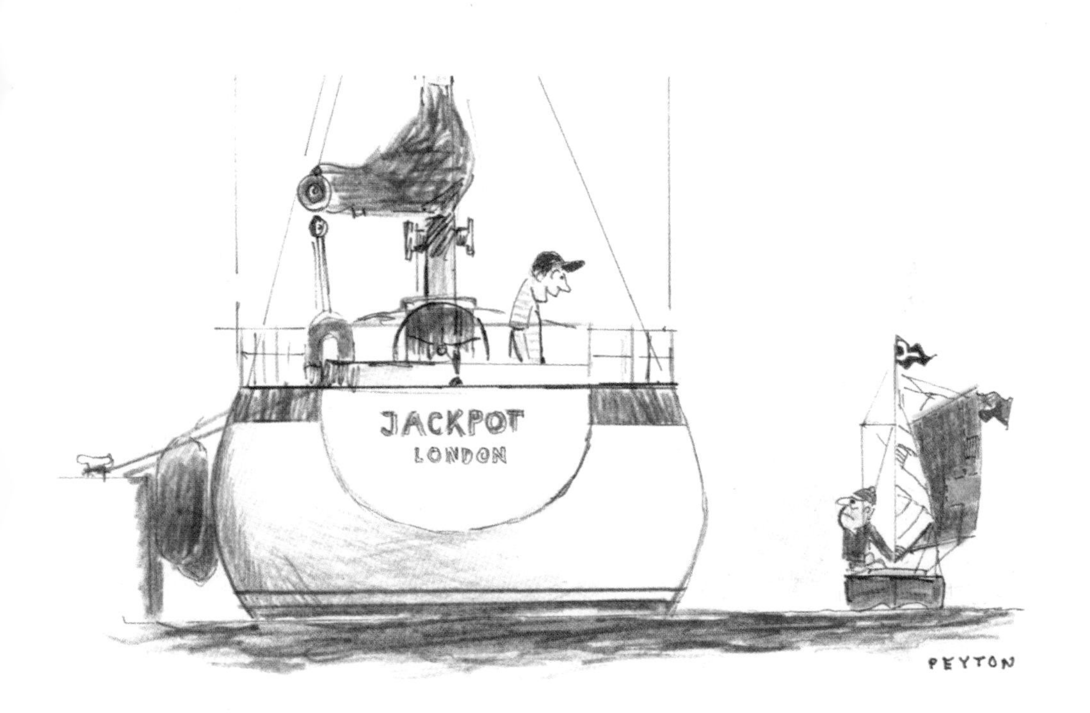

'I haven't seen you for years, Bert, how are you doing?'

'I say, old boy, would you care to come across and watch the telly?'

'She's best on a run.'

'No dear, you go and tell them we're leaving.'

'Our luck's in Pete. We can relax on a mooring like this come what may.'

'Bad luck Joe – you got out of your bunk too soon!'

'Good trip?'

'What's kept you? I've been waiting hours to pick you up.'

'That's the conical we were looking for alright....'

'They never believe me at the office.'

4

All Ashore

'Well, it says visiting yachtsmen welcome!'

'Of course I'm worried. This is his sixth visit.'

'I reckon there'll be more lying down than upstanding with this lot.'

'Look – my old boat!'

FARAWAY

'I thought your valeting service...'

'It's a wonderful forecast: gales in all areas...'

'Here's to absent friends – especially those on the Christmas cruise.'

'Yachtmaster candidates?'

'And don't bring anything back.'

'I took early retirement.'

'X9721B, X9721B, X9721B, X9721B, X9721B, X9721B...'

'I suppose this is where they magnetise them.'

'I'll give you twenty to one their drinks order is four pints of bitter.'

'It ruined my Boat Show.'

5

Jumbles

'Remember when you loved Joe like that?'

'I promise I'll be back immediately I've unloaded.'

'I'm afraid "I've been to a boat jumble" is no excuse, sir.'

'Funny, the only thing we've sold is that book on dynamic salesmanship.'

'What I'm after is a cruising chute with an 11-11.5 metre hoist, preferably in blue or green.'

'It's a deal, a straight swop – my stall for yours.'

6

Below Decks

'Oh John's fine; he's gossiping too.'

'You're always talking about the good old days, so you'd better come on watch. The batteries are flat and we've no engine, autopilot, GPS, radio, echosounder or log!'

'I know we didn't do it like this at nav. classes...'

7

Stopped for the Moment

'I can see our mast dear.'

DIEPPE
ROUEN

'As you said, we work all week to pay for our weekends of fun . . .'

'Doesn't look as if 'Deversoir' is back.'

'Fancy joining us for a beer mate?'

'It looks as if we'll just have to relax for a couple of hours dear until low water.'

'I've noticed they always do it just after the ebb starts and always in their Y-fronts.'

'It's ironic: the week you pass your Yachtmasters!'

SEA HOLLY
PEYTON

'Sometimes it's difficult to believe this is considered quality time.'